On and Off

LEVEL 1

/ff/

DECODABLES

BY jump!

Teaching Tips

Pink Level 1

This book focuses on the phoneme **/ff/**.

Before Reading

- Discuss the title. Ask readers what they think the book will be about.
- Sound out the words on page 3 together.

Read the Book

- Ask readers to use a finger to follow along with each word as it is read.
- Encourage readers to break down unfamiliar words into units of sound. Then, ask them to string the sounds together to create the words.
- Urge readers to point out when the focused phonics phoneme appears in the text.

After Reading

- Encourage children to reread the book independently or with a friend.
- Ask simple questions about the text to check for understanding. Have them find the pages that have the answers to your questions.

This edition is published by arrangement with Booklife Publishing.

5357 Penn Avenue South
Minneapolis, MN 55419
www.jumplibrary.com

Decodables by Jump! are published by Jump! Library.

Library of Congress Cataloging-in-Publication Data is available at www.loc.gov or upon request from the publisher.

ISBN: 979-8-88996-771-2 (hardcover)
ISBN: 979-8-88996-772-9 (paperback)
ISBN: 979-8-88996-773-6 (ebook)

Photo Credits

Images are courtesy of Shutterstock.com. With thanks to Getty Images, Thinkstock Photo and iStockphoto. Cover – Diabluses. 4–5 – Thanit Weerawan. 6–7 – grublee. 8–9 – Daria Minaeva. 10–11 – milatas, Rawpixel.com. 14–15 – Shutterstock.

Can you find these words in the book?

off

on

The tap is on.

The tap is off.

It is on.

It is off.

The cat is on it.

The cat is off it.

It is on.

Education Lessons
Log out
CONTENT
STUDENT LEVEL
VIDEO DURATION
All
Mathematics
Science
Language & Literature
Technology
Art & Design
History
Social Studies
Health
Philosophy & Religion
Music
States of Matters: Solid, Liquid & Gas - 06:13
How Do Our Brains Process Music? - 04:55
TECHNOLOGY
Why do Leaves Change Color? - 05:29
Technology: Changing the way we think and focus - 05:03

It is off.

Can you say this sound and draw it with your finger?

Can you say this word and draw it with your finger?

off

What other words do you know that have the letters /ff/?

earmuffs

sniff

handcuffs

coffee

Practice reading the book again:

The tap is on.

The tap is off.

It is on.

It is off.

The cat is on it.

The cat is off it.

It is on.

It is off.